Beyond the Meeting Room:

A Practical Guide to Mastering Communication in a Remote World

By

Larry Jacobson

The author welcomes comments and questions.
Please visit www.LarryJacobson.com

Published by:

BUOY
—— PRESS ——

Emeryville, California
www.BuoyPress.com
Info@BuoyPress.com
ISBN: 978-0-9828787-4-3

Other books by Larry Jacobson

The Boy Behind the Gate
How His Dream of Sailing Around the World Became a Six-Year Odyssey of Adventure, Fear, Discovery, and Love

Let's Go!
The Adventures of Skip and Kanek Part 1 -- The Search Begins

Navigating Entrepreneurship
11 Proven Keys to Success

What's Your Encore?
A Step-by-Step Guide to Retiring with Purpose and Fulfillment
(Originally Your Ideal Retirement Workbook)

All found here: www.LarryJacobson.com/author

DEDICATION

This book is dedicated to all of the remote workers of the world. You are doing yourself a big favor by reading this book and heeding some of the advice.
Stay visible!

Larry Jacobson

INTRODUCTION

Since 2019 when the Covid pandemic ruled our lives, we have been left with a world of disconnection. This book is about how to stay well-connected in an age of uncertainty about how to better communicate with each other.

Suddenly our world has been turned upside down. Personal meetings are a thing of the past and many meetings are now held using one or more of the five methods discussed here. It's no longer whether to meet in conference room number two or three, but whether to meet on zoom or google or another platform. And while these platforms are indeed convenient, they lack the real interaction of meeting in-person. So, how do we make the best of the current forms of communicating? Read on and take away some tips to at least making your end of any communication more effective.

It's not just communication that has become a bigger challenge, but also staying engaged. If you are working remotely, it can be a struggle to stay engaged with the office and the company culture. If you are managing others who are working remotely, your challenge is to keep your remote workers engaged and ensure they are tuned in to the company and its culture.

In today's world of non-personal meetings, it's easy for your words to not quite come out the way you intended.

They could be mis-interpreted (if you're lucky,) or worse yet if you're unlucky and use auto-correct, they could be interpreted as downright rude.

There's nothing quite like meeting in person. At the office, whether it be an impromptu informal meeting, or a scheduled weekly sales team meeting, it's one meeting after another. In the new Age of Remote Work, most of these meetings have been replaced with Virtual meetings. With the push to get employees back to the office, workers are finding even though everyone is "in," it has become easier to have a meeting using video conferencing.

Virtual or in-person, you still want to ensure your message is coming across the way you intended, don't you? Then read on and take away some keys to communicating better without in-person meetings.

The physical way we communicate is changing right before our eyes, and overall, we're doing a pretty good job of adapting to change. But we can do better.

Larry Jacobson

TABLE OF CONTENTS

Chapter Zero
The Way Life Used to Be

In a face to face meeting, we all pretty much know the rules.

- Raise your hand to speak
- Wait your turn if you're going around the room
- Keep your answers clear and concise
- Stay awake and attentive
- Don't eat all of the muffins

Often, in face to face meetings, agendas and goals are written on a flip chart, or pasted on the walls around the room, and the moderator checks in with, "How are we doing towards our goals?" and "What's next on our agenda?"

Meetings are usually distraction-free, and anybody walking by in the hallway speaking loudly is promptly told, "Shhh, we're in a MEETING."

In a real in-person meeting, speaking face to face with colleagues affords us luxuries we have taken for granted such as facial expressions and body language. A raised hand means a question or comment. Other hand gestures are equally important (no, not THAT kind of hand gesture) ☺

- A simple raise of the eyebrow questions a point
- Raising two eyebrows is an exclamation point
- And as we learned from the Italians, a single shoulder shrug is "eh, maybe"
- A double shoulder shrug means, "I have no idea, what the heck did you say?"

Advantages of In-Person Meetings

Visual Expressions such as:
- The Shrug
- The Raised Eyebrow
- Smiles
- The Wink

Picture yourself as the presenter at a meeting. As you're making your points, you look around the table and see arms beginning to cross, which means something is wrong and you had better address it. You are keenly aware of side conversations, which are also a bad sign you are losing the group's attention. **These things are more difficult to spot in a video meeting**.

As a professional motivational speaker I am biased towards meeting in person. I can see, hear and feel how the audience is responding to my jokes, I can see if their arms are folded, I can watch them whispering to each other, and I can see if they're texting while I'm speaking. I can also see when they move closer to the edge of their seat, and I know when they're truly listening. On the down side, there is no mute button so it's harder to deal with hecklers and interruptive questions.

On the flip side, with Virtual Speaking, if there's a heckler or an interrupting question, it's easy to deal with them. I can click "mute," answer their question in the chat box, or kick them out of the room.

The luxury of using hand and facial expressions in live meetings

I hate to be the bearer of bad news, but all of those luxuries of meeting in person are gone. The workplace has changed, and it's going to be awhile until it returns to handshakes, hugs, and other touchy-feely greetings.

Without in-person meetings, we are left with five (5) ways of meeting virtually (not counting snail mail letters) and in this book we'll look closely at each of the methods and best practices for each. For our purposes here, I do not include social media as a method of communication used for every day business. That doesn't mean it isn't important, I just don't discuss it in this book.

In chapter 8 I address practical methods for an employee to stay connected to the company. This is important for you, as you need to stay visible to stay relevant.

In the last chapter are many methods a manager can use to stay connected to the remote employee. Any company works best when the whole team works together so this is an important chapter for those managing remote workers.

There are at the moment, basically five methods of communicating without in-person meetings. I am of course leaving out smoke signals and two tin cans and a string.

5 Methods of Communication
Best Practices for Communicating Virtually

1. Texting
2. Email or Intra Office mail
3. Telephone: one-on-one or conference call
4. Video conference: one-on-one or with a group
5. Document collaboration

The Five Methods of Non-In-Person Meetings

Before we begin, let me say a word about blame, shame, guilt, and responsibility. You may see a reflection of yourself in some of the following made up scenarios. You may think, "Not me, I never do that." Or your reaction might be privately to yourself, "Oh crap, I do that." Either way, I want you to know **we have all been there**. This entire book is written based on actual experiences. It's not imaginary, which means I've done my share of some of the poorer practices we'll be talking about. THIS BOOK IS NOT ABOUT PLACING GUILT. **You're supposed to laugh at yourself, roll your eyes, and pledge to improve your communication skills.**

Let's begin

Chapter 1
Quick, Easy, and Dangerous: Texts, Messages, & SMS

Let's dive right in with overall probably the most popular form of communication today: texting. And while popular, it's fraught with potential fallout.

We all have our opinions. To me, texting feels like someone bursting into my office without knocking, jumping up on my desk, and shouting, "Talk to me—now!" It feels like that because that's what texting really is built for. "I'm running 10 minutes late, see you shortly." A text is meant to be short and immediate, that's the point. "Hey, I'm at the grocery store and there's a special on that Cabernet you like, want me to grab you one or two?"

Most people have adapted to texting and the younger the generation, the more you like it. Great! I'm learning to live with it and let's see if we can improve our texting experience for everyone. When I say texting, this could be Messages, Messenger, What'sApp, and so many others.

Here's one of the big problems with texting: When a text "pings," you don't know if it's your boss and is important, or it's your neighbor who has "Fallen, and can't get up." There's no way to know its importance until you read it, which means every time a text comes in, we all stop to read it. As a writer, I could be deep into the heart of a new creation, and I hear "ping." What if it's my nephew stranded with a broken-down car? I would stop writing for that, and offer my aid. These days though, more likely it's a meme about a politician, and while funny I'd rather see them at the time of my choosing. If I don't respond, the next text is, "Didn't you like the meme?" So, I'm obligated to be polite enough to say, "funny!" But that is another problem, because now I have engaged, and I'm fair game for receiving a slew of six more funny memes including a dancing cat.

Yes, I know I can turn off the sound or even change the sound for certain people, but what if it was my nephew stranded with a broken-down car? I haven t changed the "ping" sound for every person. I know it's the most popular method of communicating for so many people today, it merits looking closely as to how we can improve the experience for everyone.

Texting Tips

- What if I don't reply immediately?
- The never-ending conversation
- Begin text, have the conversation, finish it, and move on.
- Don't leave me hanging.
- I might be busy.

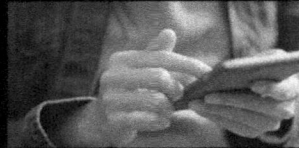

Let's take a look at some of the most common texting "issues." Please remember these are my opinions. You can agree or not. But if you do embrace many of these ways of improving, you'll make a bigger and better impression than you expect.

Like it or not, texting is definitely here to stay. Younger generations love it and so I'm all for embracing it. But all generations can improve our texting skills so no matter your age, read on. If you disagree with a point I am making, keep reading as you might agree with the next suggestion

1. **Not replying right away**, which if I don't do, gets followed by another text, "Are you there?" or, "Are you okay?" If I choose not to answer a text for any number of reasons, such as it is 2am or I'm trying to work, invariably someone thinks something is wrong. "Hey, just checking up on you," or the embedded guilt of, "You must be busy" (and not have time for little old me).

   May I humbly suggest we are not always available? Don't expect an answer about your funny meme during work hours, which for me as a writer, could be any time of day or night.

   This can be a matter of training your friends. Because I have made the mistake of always replying right away, I'm now known as a quick replier. So now if I don't reply immediately, that is usually rewarded with a, "Hey, are you okay?" According to my nephew, who is much younger than me, it's okay not to answer a text right away and that is something I am working on.

2. **The never-ending conversation** is cne of the most blatant abuses of the texting privilege. I send a text at 10am asking, "Phone call at 6pm tonight?" He replies an hour later (fine, he has his reasons to not reply right away), "Sure, call me then." Perfect, I think we're done, but ohhh no, no...we've only just begun. Because an hour later I get a text from him saying, "Did you see the news yesterday?" Thinking this could be important, I stop my train of thought, and reply, "Nc, we'll talk at 6." He then replies 2 hours later with, "There was a big battle in Afghanistan." I don't answer, so about another hour later, "Four soldiers killed." And the conversation never ends. Or you get the running corrmentary of their day such as, "My boss is such a jerk," which carries an implied request for sympathy or a discussion to find out what their boss has done now. And then an hour later, "They say it's going to rain tomorrow."

Please think of the person on the other end of your texts. They might be trying to watch a show, write, work, cook a meal, and every time you send a text, they stop, lose their momentum or train of thought, look at what you have written, and reply or not. Either way, they were interrupted. While I have not done a formal study on productivity levels since the introduction of texting, based on my own experience, they are down.

3. **The sudden drop off and much delayed response.** One evening I received a text at 9pm checking to make sure I was well. That was very nice and much appreciated. I was watching a movie so I responded an hour later that I was indeed well.

In order to ensure there wasn't going to be a conversation, I added I was watching a movie, and was then headed to the bath and bed. This was at 10pm, and I kid you not, the response came at 2am asking if I had seen the news. Why the sudden drop off? When I replied at 10pm, did they have nothing to say? Fine, then I assumed the conversation was over. But to pick it up again 4 hours later at 2am?

I have a friend who sends me texts at random times asking how I am. I think that's nice, so if I can, I reply with some information or a short story, and end with, and you? No response.

Did he put his phone down and not look at it again until the next day? Because sure enough, one or two days later, I receive "I'm okay." When the text comes in, I have no idea what he's talking about and have to re-read the thread and then pick up the conversation again.

If you begin a conversation via text, have the conversation, finish it, and move on. Please don't carry on a conversation all day or even longer. If we're in a text conversation, when you suddenly drop off with no explanation, I'm left hanging. When I call you to the mat on it the next day, if you offer the excuse, "Oh, I didn't see that," which is of course not true, then your integrity just went out the window.

Of course, you saw the text. Do you expect me to believe that all of a sudden you put your phone down and didn't look at any more of the texts coming in? Really?

4. **Not respecting what you might be doing at the moment.** If I tell someone I'm driving, they should reply, "Okay, talk later." Or, they can call me, or I can call them, but texting while driving is the best example of Darwin at work because it's as dangerous as it gets. As if the roadways weren't already dangerous enough, now by texting, you aren't even watching the road. Are you nuts?

Or, I get a text, see it's a good friend and reply "I'm on my walk." That should end it, but oh no, they fire right back with what they wanted to talk about right then. Here, I'm strict and don't engage. When I return from my walk, I phone them and I think the point is made then.

5. **The Repeater. Multiple texts all right in a row so your phone Pings until you're ready to throw it out the window. Ping!** "Hi, how are you?" **Ping!** "I'm going shopping." Ping! "I hear there's a sale on t-shirts." **Ping!** "Where did you get that t-shirt I like?" **Ping!**

"Hey, wanna go with me?" **Ping!** "I'll drive if you want." **Ping!** "C'mon, it'll be fun." **Ping!** "Let me know soon." **Ping!** "Are you busy? What are you doing?"

That all could have been in one message but because the person hasn't thought through what they're going to say, I am the recipient of their slow and agonizing thought process.

When you send a text, have a clear purpose. And speaking of purpose, how is one supposed to answer the text, "Wassup?" "Sup,"or "Hey Buddy?" What is it you want to know? Give me a hint. If you want to say, "Hi, thinking of you, did you by chance finish the book I loaned you?" then say that. Here is an actual conversation that wasted time, made it difficult to concentrate, and was just using up time my friend had, but I didn't.

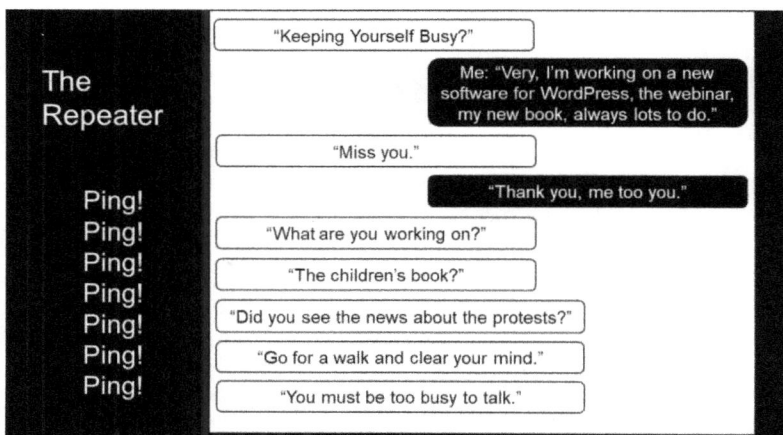

The Repeater	"Keeping Yourself Busy?"
	Me: "Very, I'm working on a new software for WordPress, the webinar, my new book, always lots to do."
	"Miss you."
Ping! Ping! Ping! Ping! Ping! Ping! Ping!	"Thank you, me too you."
	"What are you working on?"
	"The children's book?"
	"Did you see the news about the protests?"
	"Go for a walk and clear your mind."
	"You must be too busy to talk."

6. **Mistakenly** thinking you will enjoy the picture of their cat up in a tree as much as they did. **Memes** are fun, and the humor provides much needed laughter. I try to say "thanks" or send a smiley emoji, but I do so in fear of it starting a conversation I'm not ready to have at that time. Consider too that many of the memes going around have already been seen by many people, so you might not get a response at all.

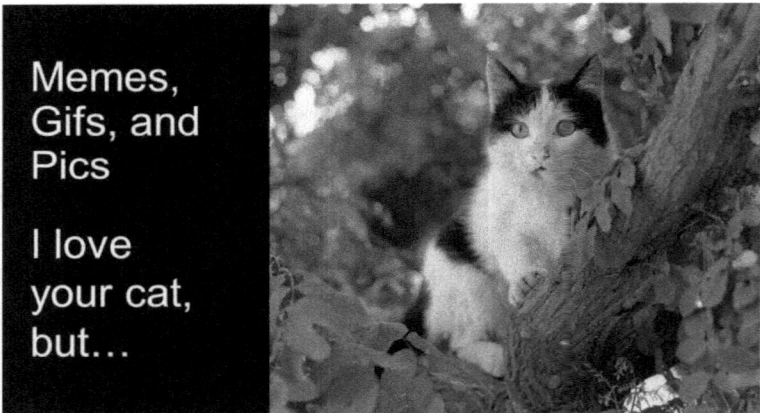

Memes, Gifs, and Pics

I love your cat, but...

7. The All Questions, No Answer person.

All Questions

No Answers

"Keeping Yourself Busy?"

Me: "Very, New webinar, new book, always lots to do. You?"

"Miss you"

"What are you working on?"

Me: "As mentioned, my new book. Need to concentrate. You?"

"The children's book?"

"Wish I could be there to help you."

"Did you see the news about the protests?

Me: "Hard to concentrate."

"Go for a walk and clear your mind."

"What are your plans tomorrow?"

"Are you having a good day?"

"I think I'll have lunch now. Did you have lunch yet?"

"You must be too busy to talk."

8. **When using Siri or dictating, remember it often auto corrects** or puts in an incorrect word, and not always to your benefit. While there can be some funny mistakes, as you see here, there are some mistakes that are shall we say, "more than funny." When using speech to text, review it before sending because what you say doesn't always end up the same on the screen. For example, has something like this ever happened to you while texting? Yes, it's funny, and hopefully everyone will laugh it off easily. However, in the business world, it's reasonable to expect you to edit before hitting "send."

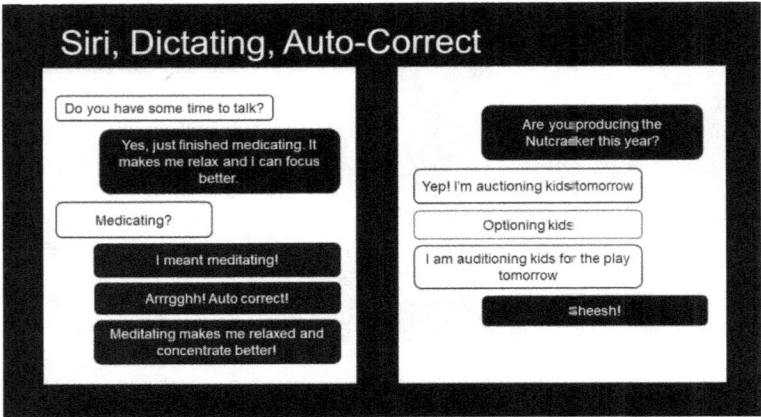
Siri, Dictating, Auto-Correct

9. **ALL CAPS SHOUTING TEXT.** For those of you who don't know this, ALL CAPS means you're SHOUTING THOSE WORDS, so unless you want to SHOUT AT ME, turn off your CAPS LOCK!

CAPS LOCK!

TURN OFF YOUR CAPS LOCK!

10. **Lacking respect for the time of day.** Some people leave their ringers on for emergency. They might have kids or nephews or nieces and want to be easily

available in case of emergency. I am one of those people so when you text me at 7am on a Saturday with a photo you found of my great uncle who was married to your mother's friend, sure enough, what I get is "Ping!" And while much younger generations might stay up late; those days are over for me. And when you wake up at 2am and decide to send me a text, sure enough, I get awakened by your "Ping!" I have now decided to turn off my ringer at night and have told my close friends how to reach me in an emergency. Google will tell you how to bypass silent mode on iPhone and the rest.

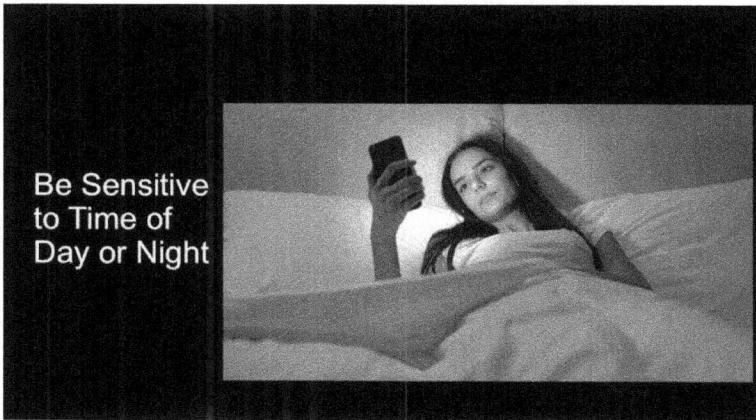

Be Sensitive to Time of Day or Night

11. **The Rambler: Similar to the Repeater but different enough to call out. Sending your stream of consciousness thoughts** on a subject in multiple rapid-fire messages, and texting your thought process in making a decision is simply a waste of time, especially mine. I sent a friend a text asking if he wanted to come over and this is the conversation that

followed. Keep in mind there's a "Ping!" with every message sent. Please do not drag me through your decision process. I have my own issues I'm dealing with, and don't need yours too. After an hour and a half of me putting off any other plans, I end up with no company for the afternoon.

"Want to come over this afternoon?"	"I still have to get a birthday present."
"Well, I have this birthday party to go to."	Five more minutes go by.
"I promised them I'd come."	"I don't have a car today, would have to take Uber."
"What time were you thinking?"	Another 10 minutes of silence.
"About 1 or 2 pm"	"You here?"
"The birthday party is at 6."	"Yes, I'm here. How about you decide and let me know"
"But it sounds fun to come over."	An hour goes by and I finally text:
And then at least 15 minutes of silence. So, I text a question.	"What did you decide?"
"What have you decided?"	"Probably not sure."
	"That's not a decision. Yes or no?"
	"What time again."
	"How about next weekend?"

The Rambler

12. **Using text to announce, "Did you get my email?"** Most, if not all of us get our emails on our phones as well as texts. While I've turned off the Ping! for email on my phone, because I'm a big emailer, I check it frequently. If you sent me an email, I'll see it. Or if it was that urgent, perhaps it should have been sent via text or an actual telephone call.

13. **Lacking a point or purpose to your text.** Ping! "It's a beautiful day outside today." How would you like me to respond to that? Would you like me to agree with or challenge you? Either way, what's next in the conversation? Where are we going with this? And then

I wait a few minutes, and nothing else comes in so I assume you just wanted to say Hi, and that it's a beautiful day outside. So, I go back to my writing and sure enough, Ping! Please have a point or purpose to your text.

Have a Point!

"It's a beautiful day outside today."

"Are you going for a walk today?"

"No, I'm doing yoga class today."

"Yoga is good."

14. **Respect the other party's wish to end the conversation.** When you send a text to start a conversation, you might have plenty of time, and you have selected when to begin. However, the other party may want to acknowledge your text, say hello, find out how you are, and then get back to what they were doing before you Pinged. When someone says, "Nice chatting, more later," or "Okay, thanks for texting, gotta run," or "Can't chat anymore, in the middle of something," please respect what they are saying. It's quite uncomfortable having to repeat over and over again that you are not available any longer, or worse is having to justify what you were doing before the text

was important enough you'd like to get back to it. Of course, this applies to telephone calls as well.

15. **How to end a text conversation.** Nobody wants to hurt another person's feelings, or cut them off, but some people have more time for text conversations than others. As mentioned, have your conversation, and then end it. But how do you end it without hurting the other party's feelings? Here are a few ways that work well. And for those who have more time to chat than the rest of us, please listen up and pay attention to the words. "Gotta go" means just that, and does not have to be justified. Examples:

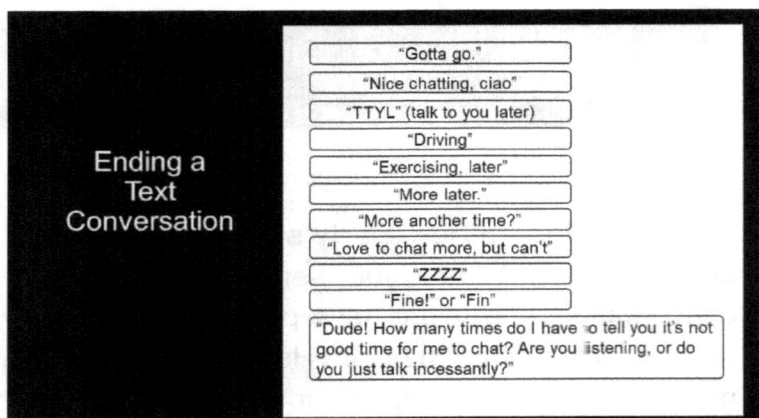

Ending a Text Conversation	"Gotta go."
	"Nice chatting, ciao"
	"TTYL" (talk to you later)
	"Driving"
	"Exercising, later"
	"More later."
	"More another time?"
	"Love to chat more, but can't"
	"ZZZZ"
	"Fine!" or "Fin"
	"Dude! How many times do I have to tell you it's not good time for me to chat? Are you listening, or do you just talk incessantly?"

16. **Group texts**, which launches a string of responses. In my humble opinion, group texts are inventions of the devil and are at the bottom of the "bad ideas" heap along with Spam and 4-way stops at intersections. Do you realize when you send a group text that it indeed goes to all of the people you named? And guess what?

20

When someone in that group responds, it again goes to all of those in the group. Then someone else responds and it goes to all the people in the group, and it goes on and on, and often you don't even know half or more of the people in the group and now you're getting Pinged all day about something you don't care about and certainly don't care to discuss with strangers. An example of how not to use group texts follows. It's easy to see why there's very little productivity with group texts.

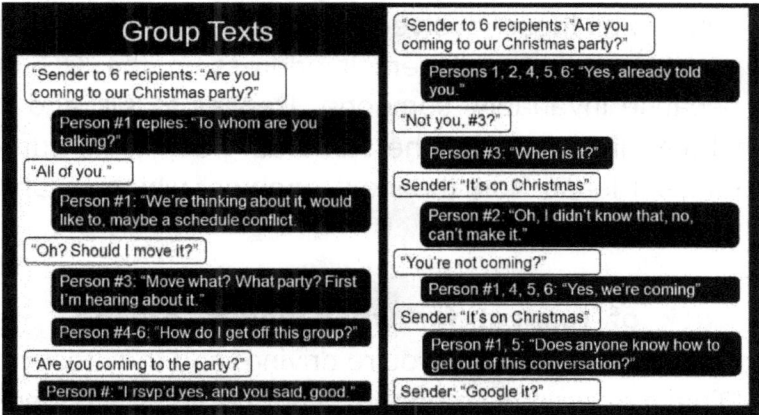

Group Texts

"Sender to 6 recipients: "Are you coming to our Christmas party?"

Person #1 replies: "To whom are you talking?"

"All of you."

Person #1: "We're thinking about it, would like to, maybe a schedule conflict.

"Oh? Should I move it?"

Person #3: "Move what? What party? First I'm hearing about it."

Person #4-6: "How do I get off this group?"

"Are you coming to the party?"

Person #: "I rsvp'd yes, and you said, good."

"Sender to 6 recipients: "Are you coming to our Christmas party?"

Persons 1, 2, 4, 5, 6: "Yes, already told you."

"Not you, #3?"

Person #3: "When is it?"

Sender; "It's on Christmas"

Person #2: "Oh, I didn't know that, no, can't make it."

"You're not coming?"

Person #1, 4, 5, 6: "Yes, we're coming"

Sender: "It's on Christmas"

Person #1, 5: "Does anyone know how to get out of this conversation?"

Sender: "Google it?"

In case you're ever caught up in one of these group texts, you will invariably want out. How to get out seems to change with the wind, and I don't want to give false information, so the only instructions I can give is to google it. Following are directions current now, and who knows when that will change. Feel free to try it as you won't "break it." On an iPhone, click on "Info" at the top of the message and then look for the "Leave conversation" button on the screen. If it's greyed out, it's most likely because the sender is on an Android phone or there are three or less participants, leaving no way out. To leave an Android group text, tap the three dots, then "Leave Chat" at the bottom of the screen. Failing that, tap the notification 'bell' to mute all future messages and notifications from that particular group. Failing that, I suggest tossing your phone into San Francisco Bay.

If you're the sender of one of these group texts, ask yourself twice if it's really necessary. As you're putting together your message, consider sending an email to all those involved. But please, if you do email, don't put everyone's email address n the CC box because invariably, someone "Replies to All" and the whole thing happens the same as group texts but via email. Please see the next chapter, which is about email.

17. **Lack of respect for when you're driving**. You respond to a text that you're driving, and they respond, "That's okay, don't respond," and then they proceed to share a story with you. As mentioned, this is the ultimate sin. If someone says they're driving, or they don't answer and you suspect they're driving, please do not bug them. You could try phoning as it's easy to answer a phone on your speaker in today's cars. Remember, if the person you're texting tries to reply, and gets in a wreck, you may not ever hear their reply.

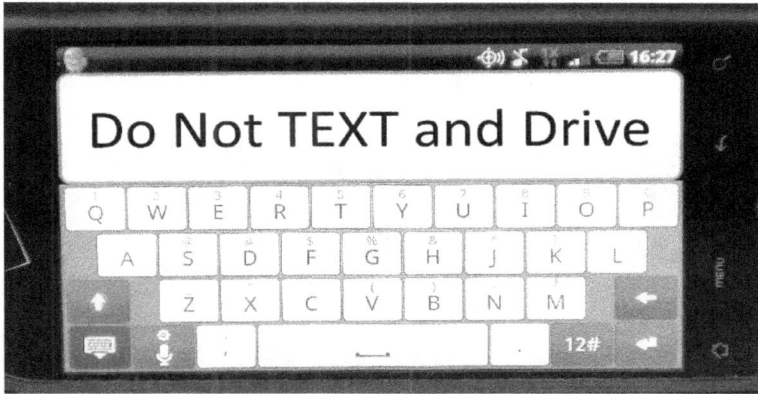

18. Ask! "Is now a good time to chat?"

Couldn't Hurt to Ask!

"Is now a good time to chat?"

19. Regarding sending **X-rated pics**

I don't give a hoot what you send. Just remember any pic sent is a pic that now somehow, is in a cloud somewhere, just waiting for the cloud to burst with your information and pics "out there." So, if your future plans involve running for public office, you might want to consider keeping your private pics to yourself.

X-Rated Pics

"Promise you won't show this to anyone else? I'm planning on running for Congress."

20. Address all issues brought up in texts and emails.
Have you ever sent a text with a few questions in it, only to get a response which answers only one of the questions? If the other questions were important, then you have to re-send another text with the same questions again. Usually you'll receive something like, "Oh, didn't see those questions." Really? You didn't? Yes, you did.

Address All Issues Brought Up

"Camping sounds fun this weekend. A few questions. Do I need to bring my own stove or will we share with the group? How do we go about getting the permit for the campsite. And, are you planning to leave Friday afternoon or Saturday morning?"

"I'd like to leave Friday night, what do you think?"

"Friday sound good. What about my questions re: campsite and stove?"

"Oh, didn't see those."

How would I like to reply:

"What do you mean you didn't see those questions? They were before the one you answered."

"Chill man, so I didn't read it all, what's the big deal?"

And then I'd like to say this:

"What's the big deal? The big deal is you're lying. You had to have read them before the other question."

21.   **Use of emojis is enjoyed by some.** I use the smiley face, the laughing face, and the ZZZZZZ to indicate I'm off to bed and can't chat. My use of an emoji usually indicates I don't want to chat because otherwise I would use words rather than a cartoon drawing. I recognize that sometimes an emoji has just the right expression you're looking for, but what's the problem, are words just too long?

Chapter 2
The "Paper Trail" You Leave Lasts Forever: Email

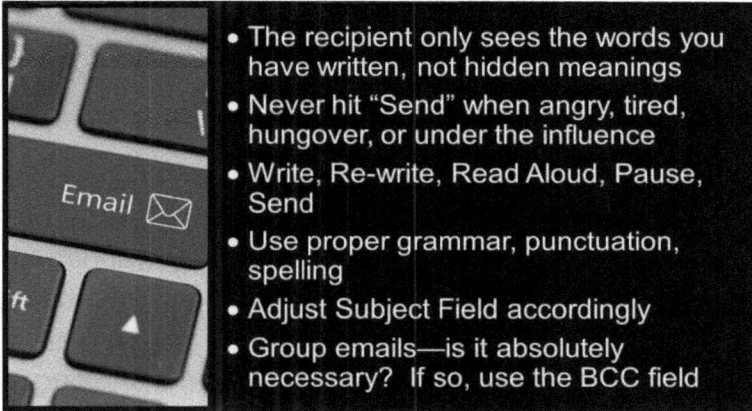

- The recipient only sees the words you have written, not hidden meanings
- Never hit "Send" when angry, tired, hungover, or under the influence
- Write, Re-write, Read Aloud, Pause, Send
- Use proper grammar, punctuation, spelling
- Adjust Subject Field accordingly
- Group emails—is it absolutely necessary? If so, use the BCC field

Have you ever sent an email and then wished you hadn't? Emails rely solely on the written word. Once you hit send, you can't pull it back (I do know that in Gmail and Macmail, you have up to 30 seconds to change your mind about sending it, but who knows after just half a minute?). Once the email has landed in someone's mailbox, you can't say, "That's not what I meant."

With Email you are creating a "paper trail" of your conversations with the other party. This can be good or bad depending on the subject at hand, so remember what you write is as good as carved in stone.

So, take your time to get it right. Here are some tips for emailing:

1. **Write exactly what you mean.** As with texting, you can add an LOL or ☺ here and there, but emojis aren't generally used in emails. Since there is no voice inflection, no visual clue as to what you really mean, choose your words carefully. To ensure you see just what the recipient sees, CC yourself. This makes it easier for you to follow the entire thread of the conversation.

2. **Never hit the send button when angry**, tired, or under the influence of anything. Has this ever happened to you? You get an email, your anger flares, and you type out a nasty response. You know when you're writing it, you aren't really going to send it, you're just using it to blow off some steam. And then, as if divine intervention, you hit send and even if you have the 30 second option, it takes you that long to even recognize what you've done.

   Here's a tip: When typing that email, remove the name from the address field. That way, if you really do want to send it, you would have to re-enter the address, and that will make you stop and think. Then sleep on your email. There's nothing like a fresh set of eyes in the morning and a new attitude to realize how glad you are you didn't send that angry email the evening before. Also, emails received in the morning are being seen by freshly rested eyes rather than tired eyes at the end of the day. This goes for texting as well.

3. **Write, Re-write, Pause, Send.** Try not to send emails at the end of your day when you've accumulated all the crap that's happened to you during the day. Often this attitude ends up in your email giving the false impression of you being a jerk. There are no take-backs. Wait until morning, re-read, re-write, and then send. You'll be glad you did, and chances are, if it's work-related, it wasn't going to be read the night before anyway.

4. **Remember there is no such thing as good writing, only good re-writing.** Take the time to use proper grammar, punctuation, and spelling. Come on, are you really in that much of a hurry that you can't capitalize a letter, start a new paragraph, or bother to find out if you spelled the recipient's name correctly? Read your email aloud and hear how it sounds. Picture the recipient opening and reading it. What will they think? How will they hear it?

5. **Adjust Subject Field Accordingly** Don't keep sending responses back and forth to each other using the same email subject. Even if you just add a "2" or "3" to the subject, it helps keep them all straight. If your first email subject was, "Restaurant recommendation" and three emails later, you're confirming the date and time, then change the email subject to "Dinner at Chez Luis Friday April 24, 7pm".

6. **Rename Word Documents with updated names.** If you make edits and changes, then change the name of the document by adding V2 or V3.

This is how your email SHOULD NOT look

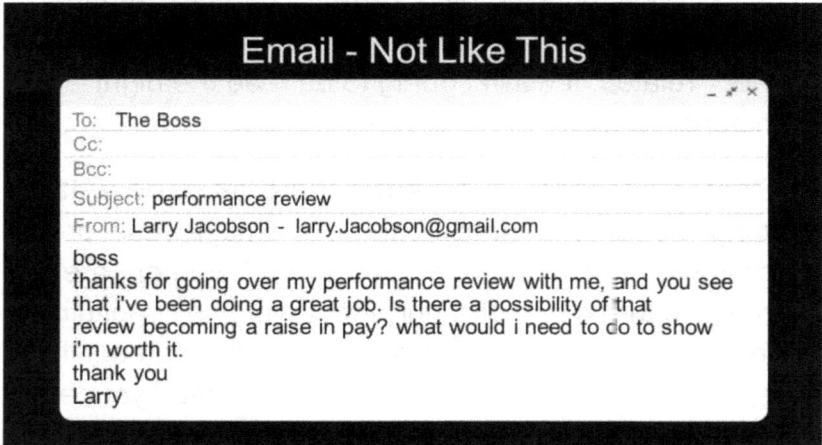

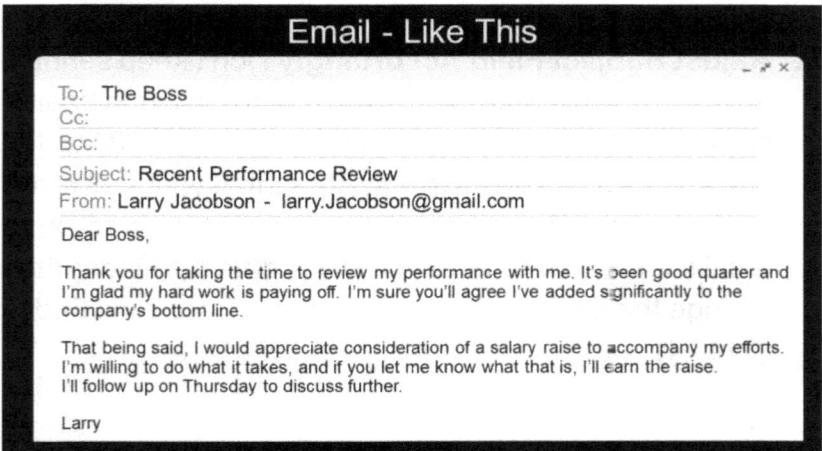

Email - Not Like This

To: The Boss
Cc:
Bcc:
Subject: performance review
From: Larry Jacobson - larry.Jacobson@gmail.com

boss
thanks for going over my performance review with me, and you see that i've been doing a great job. Is there a possibility of that review becoming a raise in pay? what would i need to do to show i'm worth it.
thank you
Larry

This is how your email SHOULD look

Email - Like This

To: The Boss
Cc:
Bcc:
Subject: Recent Performance Review
From: Larry Jacobson - larry.Jacobson@gmail.com

Dear Boss,

Thank you for taking the time to review my performance with me. It's been good quarter and I'm glad my hard work is paying off. I'm sure you'll agree I've added significantly to the company's bottom line.

That being said, I would appreciate consideration of a salary raise to accompany my efforts. I'm willing to do what it takes, and if you let me know what that is, I'll earn the raise. I'll follow up on Thursday to discuss further.

Larry

7. **Group emails.** Please don't, but if you must, send the email to yourself and put all of the group addresses in BCC (blind copy). This protects the email address privacy of all those receiving the email. It also prevents someone from clicking "Reply All," which puts you on a string of endless emails from strangers discussing a subject with which you have already finished thinking. I just received a Happy Easter email from a friend who CC'd 47 other people and now I'm receiving "Happy Easter to you too" emails from people I don't know, about a subject very low on my priority list.

If you want everybody to know who else was copied in the email, At the bottom of the body of the email, take the extra time to write: "This email also sent to Terry, Bob, Bill, Susan, Laura, and Richard." You can use their last names if you wish, but it's not your place to be putting their email addresses out into the world of email abuse and potential spam.

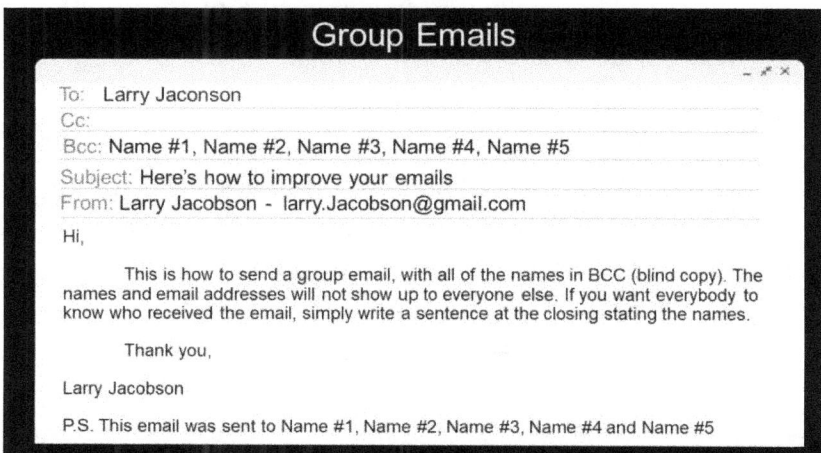

Group Emails

To: Larry Jaconson
Cc:
Bcc: Name #1, Name #2, Name #3, Name #4, Name #5
Subject: Here's how to improve your emails
From: Larry Jacobson - larry.Jacobson@gmail.com

Hi,

    This is how to send a group email, with all of the names in BCC (blind copy). The names and email addresses will not show up to everyone else. If you want everybody to know who received the email, simply write a sentence at the closing stating the names.

    Thank you,

Larry Jacobson

P.S. This email was sent to Name #1, Name #2, Name #3, Name #4 and Name #5

8. **Email wars** can happen when you start arguing over some petty little thing, or you misunderstand something, or you or they mis-interpret something. If this happens, then STOP emailing, and pick up the phone. Only a conversation can clear up written messes. They or you have to hear they/you really misunderstood or read something wrong. You have to hear that in the voice, and that's just a phone call away.

9. **When is the best time and day to send emails?** It depends on what you're sending. I believe emails sent for personal reasons are best sent on the weekend. Most people aren't burdened with the stress of work and are in a more relaxed mood and can take the time to read your message.

   If you're sending a sales pitch email, avoid Mondays and Fridays. Mondays for obvious reasons of catching up, grumpiness, and the urgency of taking care of current items on lists rather than thinking about buying new things or programs.

   If follow up is required or you're expecting a response, send a second email no more than a week after the first. I prefer to follow up with a second email two or three days after the first, and then again after another three or four days. After that, a couple of weeks later, and if no response, I'll add a phone call into the mix.

- Remember, when emailing, you must say what you mean because all the reader has to go on, is your words.
- If your email is subject to interpretation, that's your responsibility

Email Reminder

- When emailing, you must say what you mean because all the reader has is your words.

- If your email is subject to interpretation, that's your responsibility.

Chapter 3
Smile! You're On Camera:
Video Conferencing

The latest and greatest form of communicating in the absence of a face to face meeting is live video. The technology has grown by leaps and bounds and now that the internet can keep up with the demand on traffic, it's rapidly replacing face to face meetings. One ad more than a few years ago for GoToMeeting showed a salesman waiting in line to go through airport security and then another line to board the plane, a delayed flight and other hassles of travel. The caption on the ad read: "The Ultimate Upgrade—Don't Go." Live Video says, "There's no need to go."

GoToMeeting, Zoom, WebEx, Google Meet, Facetime, What's App, there are many to choose from depending on your needs. We'll use Zoom as the example.

Meeting Participants & Hosts

Dress the Part	Look at Yourself	Look at the Camera
Be On Time	Lighting	Smile
Be Professional	Sound	Be present
Mute	Background	
Chat	Posture	

Here are some tips on how best to participate in any video call or meeting.

1. **Dress the part.** Just because you're working from home, doesn't mean you should dress like a slob. **Everyone knows the world is more casual now, but the image you present, is the image they remember. Put on a nice shirt or whatever your company culture calls** for, but avoid busy checks and stripes. Shower, shave, groom, have your coffee and water ready at your desk. Preparing yourself physically helps prepare you mentally. Getting dressed and ready for a meeting convinces your subconscious mind you are truly in a real meeting.

2. **Show up on time.** Actually, on time is late. Be early. Enough said.

3. **Be Professional. Go to the bathroom ahead of the meeting.** If you're hosting a meeting longer than an hour, give your attendees a bathroom break. Speaking of the bathroom, if you are so bold as to risk going to the bathroom, please remember to mute yourself as a flushing toilet can be very loud. ☺

   Your cat, dog, or baby is cute, but if it's **a business meeting, you're there to do business.** And calling for one of the kids or your partner to "Please come and get Taffy" is a total interruption to the host of the meeting. Clear your time and space ahead of time. If it's an online dance party of course, use your imagination!

4. On a similar subject, **mute yourself** except when called upon to speak. Some of the programs allow you to "raise your virtual hand" to ask a question. In Zoom, if you want to say something and you are muted, simply press the space bar on your keyboard to speak, release to mute again. If you do not mute yourself, the rest of the meeting is subject to hearing your husband doing the dishes, your keyboard clicks, the unwrapping of your Snickers bar, and all of these add up to make a very annoying background for whomever is speaking at the time.

5. **Use the chat box** to ask a question to the group or send a private message to someone else in the meeting. The host never sees your private chats.

Know Your Dashboard

6. **Whispering** to a colleague next to you in a face-to-face meeting is not polite, but does happen. We know not to have private whisper conversations out of respect for the presenter. Having a side conversation in a video meeting means everybody hears while you interrupt the

presenter. It's a big no-no, so use the chat box if you must whisper about Bob and Dana's hot romance.

7. **Adjust your camera accordingly.** If you plan on standing during the meeting, or if you happen to have a big mirror on the wall behind you, then I strongly suggest you **wear pants** as well as the top part of your outfit. On this subject, I definitely speak from experience.

8. **Look at your background.** A plain background is best, but a home office showing a bookcase and a couple of awards makes it a bit more personal and reflects who you are. Avoid showing us too many of your family photos and Knick knacks. A room divider screen makes a great background. With Zoom, you can upload a photo to use as your virtual background.

   If you have a low bandwidth though, this will cause a choppy video and pixilation of you over the background image. If using a virtual background, try to use one that is somewhat relevant and reflects who you are without being too distracting. You want the other party to focus on you, not the background.

9. **Proper lighting is important.** Light your face from the front, overhead, or sides, but be careful not to light one side of your face while putting the other side in a shadow. If you wear glasses, remember you will get a reflection of them on your screen.

This is a video meeting for a reason—so the host and others can see your pretty face. They will also see your smile, your eyes, and your expressions and reactions.

If you have a window behind you, close the curtains or blinds as light behind you will make your face too dark to see. Test how you look and how your background and lighting look by doing a test on zoom, or on a Mac, you can use Photo Booth to test how you look. Note how the lighting changes as the meeting progresses. If it's getting dark, be prepared with more lighting, or you and your ideas will fade into the darkness.

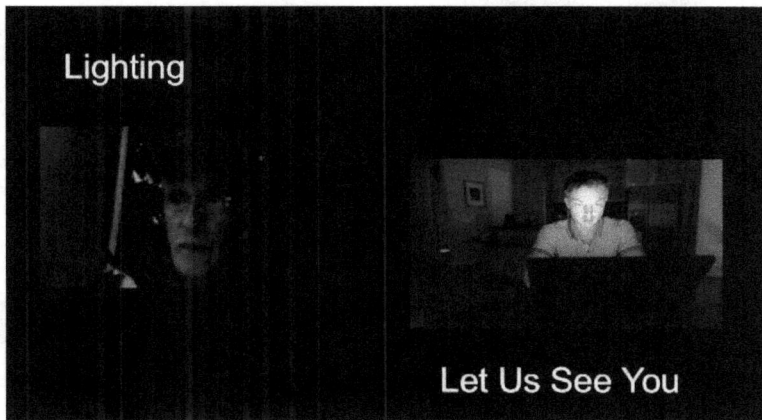

These people looked good at the beginning of the meeting, but as the afternoon faded into evening, they faded into the evening and from our minds.

10. **Look and listen to yourself** in the meeting and see what others are seeing. **CHECK YOUR POSTURE**. If you're on a laptop and it's well below your face and

pointing up, you're going to add a chin or two to your face. Try to keep the camera at your eye level. If you're looking down, chances are you are showing the top of your head more than your smiling face.

Know where your camera and microphone are on your computer. If you're used to covering up your camera with a sticky note, when you move it to the side, be sure you're not covering your microphone. Speaking of microphones, if you spend a lot of time on video, invest in a decent microphone and camera to override the ones built in to your computer.

Your Camera and Microphone Settings

11. **Smile.** Yes, smile, it's contagious.

12. **Be present. Act interested.** Fake it if you have to. There's a lot of pressure on the host to hold a good meeting. Respect that.

13. **Look at the camera.** If you look at your monitor and all the activity that's happening in a toolbar at the

bottom of the screen, and your camera is at the top of your computer, it will always seem as though you're looking down. Make a conscious effort to look directly at the camera, especially when speaking.

14. Have a **pen and paper** ready to take notes.

15. Learn how to **share your screen** and use the chat box.

Chapter 4
For Meeting Hosts

More For Meeting Hosts

- Set Tone of Meeting
- Present Agenda
- Send Handouts Beforehand
- Briefly remind how to use Chat, Mute, etc
- Keep Attendees Tuned in and Engaged
- Breakout Rooms

When you are the meeting host, your presence comes with a bit more responsibility. Everyone attending is hoping it will be a good and productive meeting. So, do some homework and make it so.

1. **You set the tone of the meeting.** Is it the first of a series, what kind of interaction are you looking for? Do you want feedback? Will you be taking questions? Will you use breakout rooms? Or is this an announcement? **Be sure to start and end on time.**

2. **Have a meeting goal and / or agenda.** It doesn't have to be written, but at least state the goal or agenda at the beginning of the meeting. Come back to it as often as you need to with, "Let's try to stick to our agenda," or "How are we doing toward our goal?"

Have an Agenda

Meeting Agenda

May 28, 2020
• 5pm-6pm
• Zoom with standard company ID #

• Check in to see how each person is doing
• Create Holiday Party committee
• Set schedule for reporting
• Announce promotions
• Announce bonuses

3. **If you have handouts**, distribute them before the meeting via email so you don't have to take the time to do so during the meeting. If you don't want the audience seeing each of your handouts until it's "time" for their turn, you can have the handouts up on a webpage for download, or have pre-set emails you can just hit one "click" and off it goes.

4. **Remind attendees** about the chat box, to mute themselves, and how to unmute themselves if called upon.

5. **Keep your attendees tuned in**, engaged, give them something interesting so they don't have to fake interest. If they seem to be drifting away, ask yourself why?

6. **Check in with attendees** by polling them on subjects. "Let's go around the room and get some feedback on that idea."

7. **End with next steps** and assignments, as well as a next meeting date if possible.

8. **Breakout Rooms** can be effective, but are a challenge. Be sure each breakout room has a leader in charge of summarizing the mini-group's findings and is then responsible for reporting back to the main group a brief summary. Set an exact time for the groups to re-join the main group. Watch the tutorials on this.

9. It's a good practice to **have a tech backup person** in the meeting with you, especially for meetings with more than 10 or so people. The tech hero can help attendees with mute, chat, screen sharing, and the rest of the technology, while you run the meeting. Be sure to assign them as co-host of the meeting.

10. **Watch the tutorials.** All of the services have their own tutorials and you can learn great tips and tricks in just a few minutes. You want to be able to focus on the meeting itself, not the technology. For example, Zoom has free live classes and video tutorial.

Chapter 5
We Can Still Talk to Each Other:
Telephone & Voicemail

The telephone is one of the greatest inventions ever created. Is it my imagination or does it seem to be fading away like in-person meetings? The phone used to be hands down my first choice for any communication purpose, but nowadays many people don't answer their phones, nor do they listen to voicemail. Let's have a closer look.

1. **If you want to talk, pick up the phone and call. If I'm busy, I'll let it roll to VOICEMAIL.** If you don't leave a voicemail, I'll assume you had nothing to say and didn't want to talk, although then I'm not sure why you would have called in the first place. It's not my responsibility to check my "missed calls", call you back, and ask "Did you call? What did you want to talk about?" And I'm going to scream if I hear one more time, "Nothing, it wasn't important." If you just wanted to say, "Hi" that's fine and much appreciated. It's not "nothing." And if you don't reach me, leave a voicemail that says, "Was just thinking of you."

2. **VOICEMAIL** is one of the best inventions ever, and these days it's passé to use it. Why? It is the under-used miracle. By leaving a voicemail, you get to tell me your call was important and exactly the reason why. If I have to scan my calls, see that you called, then call you

back not knowing what you were calling about, do you see how that just adds a huge step in the communication process? Sorry millennials, you don't know what you're missing. Yes, boomers invented voicemail (originally as the answering machine) because it works. When you leave a message, the listener gets to hear the purpose of your call, your voice inflection, tone, and sense of urgency or not. You don't have to tell the entire story of why you're calling-- leave a teaser and make it short and sweet.

3. **What time of day should you phone?** This is generally how the typical business day goes:
   - The first hour of everyone's day is spent organizing and preparing for the flow of the day. So, 8 to 9, or 9 to 10 are not good times to call.
   - Between 10am and noon are working hours.
   - Noon to 1pm is lunch.
   - 1pm to 2pm is either a real nap or wishing for one
   - 2pm to 5pm are working hours.
   - Higher level executives are best to reach between 4pm and 7pm as they tend to stay later. Also, their assistants are often gone by 5:30pm or 6pm, and they're left to answer their own phones.

I encourage use of the telephone and voicemail. It's quick, efficient, and you get to know each other through tone and inflection of your voice. Surprise someone—leave them a voicemail!

Telephone & Voicemail

What Time of Day to Call?
- Between 10am-noon
- Between 2pm -5pm
- Executives between 4pm and 7pm
- The Under-used Miracle
- Voicemail

Chapter 6
Watch Me Edit Your Work:
Document Collaboration

Document Collaboration can be very effective for gathering the opinions and expertise of multiple people.

- If you're asked to collaborate on a document, jump right in with your ideas.
- However, don't make changes just to show you made a change.
- You can also compliment the author and say, "It looks good to me!"
- Be polite
- Be patient
- Don't be sarcastic

Document Collaboration

- If you're the Document Creator/Owner, Set the Timeline
- Be Specific with what kind of input you seek
- Follow the Timeline set by document owner
- Silence is acquiescence

Key Points

1. **If you're the document creator or owner**, and want feedback and suggestions, ask for them, and set a timeline for submission.

2. **Be specific** with what kind of input you seek. Do you need a grammar check? Need someone to check your math? Document layout?

3. **Follow the timeline** for requested changes and suggestions. If you need more time, ask the document owner/creator.

4. **Silence is acquiescence**. Don't complain later if you choose not to participate now.

5. **Don't tell someone** they don't know what they're talking about. Instead, ask for backup of their point, you might learn something new.

6. **Don't put people down** for presenting ideas you don't like. Sharing an idea of any sort is better than not participating at all. There's always a little silver lining in just about any idea.

7. **Don't assume** that because your document is available, that it will be read and worked on. Everybody has their own priorities.

Collaboration on a document can be a great experience, and can attract new and better ideas. Or it can turn into a bad experience. Do your part to make it good for as many as possible.

Document collaboration is a great new way to create lists, get opinions, and let others in on the creation of an idea. Be prepared though, some people like yours truly who is a writer, find the idea of someone changing my edits right before my eyes is a bit hard to handle. But, collaboration is growing on me.

Chapter 7
Back to Basics

Here are **9 Keys to Effective Communication** that apply to virtual or in person, but are especially important with virtual communication. No matter when or how you're meeting, if you keep these 9 Keys to Good Communication close to your heart, you'll be seen as a positive addition to any meeting.

9 Keys to Effective Communication

1. Respect the other person including their opinion and position
2. Have clear intentions for what results you want
3. Be clear in your statements and questions.

1. **Respect** the other person including their opinion and position. This goes for your whole life filled with virtual and in-person engagements.

2. **Be clear** with your intentions to yourself and others. Be specific.

3. **Be clear** with your statements and questions. The more specific you are, the closer those answers will lead to your goals and intentions.

4. **Anticipate** questions and objections. If you were hearing your presentation for the first time, what questions and objections would you have? If you have thought of it, chances are someone else has also.

5. **Active Listening** doesn't just mean waiting for your turn to speak. Listen intently and give feedback such as, "Tell me more" or "Go on." When you respond, only do so after you have digested what the other person said. Pause, think for a moment while putting your answer together, and then speak. Don't just blurt out what you were going to say just so you can get your two cents in. A conversation is a two-way affair, it's not a monologue. If you are a talker, be aware of that, and pause occasionally in case someone else wants to jump into the conversation. Ask yourself, "WAIT," or "Why am I talking?"

   The next four keys to effective communication are commonly used by many groups as standard advice. And while they are not new, they are very important.

6. **Is it the truth?** This should be rather obvious, and I believe that one little lie leads you down a path full of thorns. If you lie you might not remember what you said before and being caught lying can really damage your credibility.

7. **Is it beneficial?** Or is it just junk you overheard, Will it benefit everyone who hears it? Even if you think something is beneficial and will help some people, but will hurt others, don't say it.

8. **Is it important?** Is it important that something be said? Is it relevant to the conversation you are currently having or is it something out of right field?

9. **Is it timely?** Is it really important that be said right now? If you are part of a team just about to give a big presentation, is it really important to mention right now that Kevin's dog died over the weekend? Couldn't it wait?

4. Anticipate questions and objections
5. Active listening: Put as much effort into listening as you do when speaking
6. Is it the truth?
7. Is it beneficial?
8. Is it important?
9. Is it timely?

Chapter 8
How to Stay Engaged with Your Company from Afar

The aftermath of the pandemic left changes in the workplace. Specifically, the place we work, as many people are still working from home. On one hand, this new place of work offers convenience, flexibility and autonomy. However, there's a reason it's called remote as it is away from the office and it can feel isolating to the worker. And if as a remote employee, you remain too remote, the company may have a hard time remembering who you are and why you are with the company. Staying engaged with your company isn't just about logging in every day—it's about making intentional efforts to connect, communicate, and contribute. As a remote employee, you can take charge of your engagement by building relationships, participating in company culture, and showing initiative. Here's how:

1. Communicate Proactively

- **It's important to be Visible in Virtual Spaces:** This means actively participating in team meetings, virtual coffee chats, and online discussions. Simple actions like turning on your camera during video calls will create a stronger sense of presence and give you a stronger feeling of belonging.

- **Check-In Regularly:** Don't wait for your manager to reach out. Proactively provide updates on your work and ask about team priorities and how you and your team are progressing toward stated company goals and objectives. You can also make your presence more well-known by showing genuine interest in your colleagues' projects and offering assistance if possible.

2. Participate in Cultural Activities

- **Engage in Team-Building Events:** If you are working remotely, it is even more important to attend virtual happy hours, trivia games, and online social gatherings. Even if you're introverted, showing up makes a difference. If you can get into the office for these events, that's even better.

- **Celebrate Company and Employee Milestones:** Acknowledge birthdays, work anniversaries, company milestones, and team achievements in company chat groups or meetings. Take the initiative on this, even volunteering to organize or lead a virtual celebration event.

3. Leverage Technology

- **Stay Active on Communication Platforms:** Precisely because you work remotely, it is expected that you will be proficient in the use of tools like Slack, Microsoft Teams, or Zoom side to side groups, even those which are just informal conversations.

- **Share Content:** Just like with social media, the more you post, the more visible you are. Post interesting articles, industry insights, or team-related information in appropriate channels to contribute to workplace culture. Don't go overboard and look like a kiss-ass, but be visible enough to keep you known in a good light.

4. Show Appreciation

- **Recognize Others:** Praising colleagues for their accomplishments, and for helping you in team projects goes a long way towards being seen. Give them shout outs in meetings, chat groups, and wherever else these will be noticed.

- Likewise, **sending a simple 'thank you'** message or email can go a long way in strengthening relationships. When you appreciate others, they will appreciate you right back.

5. Align with Company Values

- **You're part of the company—show it.** Without acting like a high-school cheerleader, reference company goals, mission, and core values in your communications. Use your company signature on your internal as well as external emails.

- **Be a Company Advocate:** When appropriate, share good company news, achievements, and successes on social media to show your pride in the organization. Showing you are proud of where you work goes a long way with management.

6. Seek Feedback and Contribute

- **Ask for Feedback:** Request input on your performance and involvement. To continuously improve, don't just ask, but act on the feedback and make the improvements. At your next evaluation, point to the suggestions and how you tackled them and succeeded or not. This is very impressive to a reviewer.

- **Propose New Ideas:** Contribute to projects that align with your skills and interests to demonstrate your engagement.

7. Build Meaningful Relationships

- Find a Mentor or Buddy: Establish deeper connections by seeking guidance from a senior colleague or manager.

- Schedule Virtual Coffee Chats: Set up informal one-on-one meetings with team members to learn more about them and their roles.

8. Keep Learning and Growing

- Attend Training Sessions: Engage in company-provided learning opportunities like webinars and workshops.

- Suggest Learning Topics: Recommend subjects for team learning sessions and share insights from classes you may be taking.

As a remote worker, you must deliver high-quality work consistently. Ultimately, engagement isn't just about communication—it's about showing dedication through the work you deliver. Meet deadlines, stay reliable, and demonstrate enthusiasm to reinforce your role as a valuable team member.

By implementing these strategies, you'll not only feel more connected to your company but also position yourself as an engaged, proactive team player who belongs at the company.

Chapter 9
How to Keep Your Remote Workers Engaged

For managers leading remote teams, engagement isn't just a "nice-to-have"—it's essential for productivity, retention, and team morale. Creating a strong sense of connection requires deliberate actions to foster communication, collaboration, and company culture. Here's how you can keep your remote employees engaged and motivated:

1. Foster Regular Communication

- **Set Up Consistent Check-Ins**: Weekly or bi-weekly meetings help maintain alignment and personal connection. They also provide consistent reminders to the remote workers they actually do work for a company. A good example of this is a Monday morning sales meeting.

- **Encourage Open Dialogue:** Create a culture where employees feel comfortable sharing concerns, ideas, and updates.

2. Build a Strong Team Culture

- **Plan Virtual Team-Building Activities:** Engage employees with activities such as:

- Virtual escape rooms
- Online trivia competitions
- Show & Tell sessions
- Themed dress-up days for video calls
- Virtual coffee chats or happy hours

- **Encourage Non-Work Interactions:** Set up casual chat channels for hobbies, pets or personal interests.

3. Provide Clear Purpose and Vision

- **Align Work with Company Goals:** Regularly communicate how employees' contributions impact the bigger picture.

- **Reinforce Company Values:** Integrate values into meetings, recognition programs, and team discussions. Many companies brag about their up to date policies encouraging individuality and diversity. Keep these alive whenever you have the opportunity.

4. Leverage Collaboration Tools

- **Use Digital Workspaces:** Platforms like Slack or Microsoft Teams keep teams connected.

- **Enable Easy Access to Information:** Make sure employees can quickly find resources, policies, and project updates.

5. Recognize and Appreciate Contributions

- **Celebrate Achievements:** Publicly acknowledge successes in meetings, newsletters, or chat groups.

- **Send Personalized Notes or Small Gifts:** A simple thank-you message, digital gift card, or care package really boosts morale.

6. Offer Flexibility

- **Support Work-Life Balance:** Allow flexible hours when possible and encourage breaks to prevent burnout.

- **Trust Your Team:** Give employees autonomy over their schedules and work styles. If the work is not getting done, then you may have to revisit this.

7. Encourage Learning and Development

- **Offer Professional Growth Opportunities:** Provide access to online courses, mentorship programs, coaching, and internal training.

- **Create a Knowledge-Sharing Culture:** Host skill-sharing sessions where employees teach each other valuable skills. This will help prevent a wisdom walkout.

8. Maintain Strong Leadership Presence

- **Hold Monthly "All-Hands" Meetings:** Keep employees informed about company updates, goals, and achievements.

- **Be Approachable and Transparent:** Foster trust by being open about challenges, strategies, and future plans. Gossip spreads like wildfire in a company, so you may as well get it out there the way you want.

9. Implement Thoughtful Communication Strategies

- **Daily or Weekly Stand-Ups:** Quick team check-ins ensure everyone is aligned and supported.

- **Asynchronous Updates:** Allow team members in different time zones to contribute without needing real-time meetings. Getting someone in Mumbai to meet with someone in New York can be a challenge.

- **Encourage Feedback Loops:** Use anonymous surveys or open forums for employees to voice suggestions and concerns.

10. Make Work Fun and Engaging

- **Create a Team Playlist:** Have employees contribute their favorite songs for a shared music experience.

- **Organize Virtual Cooking or Craft Classes:** Host creative sessions where employees can bond beyond work tasks.

- **Run Fitness or Wellness Challenges:** Promote team well-being through step challenges, meditation sessions, or group workouts.

By prioritizing communication, recognition, and meaningful engagement strategies, you'll foster a connected and motivated remote workforce. Strong engagement leads to increased productivity, job satisfaction, and long-term retention—making your company a place where remote employees feel truly valued.

Chapter 10
Final Thoughts

I for one, miss live meetings. But if we look at virtual meetings as opportunity, they can be a lot of fun and you can shine!

Summary

- Be Yourself
- Share the Opportunity to Participate
- This is Your Chance to Become a Great Communicator
- Spread the Word about the Best Practices Learned Here
- Don't Be Afraid of Virtual Communications
- Make it Work for You!

Communicating while we are in a Remote World is now far more important than ever. There really aren't good replacements for hand gestures, voice tone, voice inflection, and all of the other beautiful things about meeting in-person. If you are/were an outgoing personality with good in-person communication skills, your challenge is to continue being yourself without being the only one who speaks in a zoom meeting. If you are/were more of an introverted personality who struggled with in-person meetings, then this is your chance to become the great communicator overnight.

Remember to laugh at yourself, roll your eyes, and pledge to improve your communication skills.

USE these best practices for communicating, and pass the word when you see things being hand ed incorrectly. Together, we can bring the world together through virtual communication.

Connect with Larry on Social Media

- www.linkedin.com/in/larryjjacobson
- www.facebook.com/YourUnstoppableLife
- www.LarryJacobson.com
- www.OwnTheStage.org
- Instagram: LarryJacobsonAuthor

About the Author
Larry Jacobson
Leadership & Speaking Coach

A sought after and seasoned business and personal coach, and mentor to aspiring leaders, Jacobson uses his success in 20 years of business, including becoming a CEO, and then achieving his personal dream of sailing around the world as a model to help his clients reach their goals. His experience has attracted clients from entrepreneurs, to CEO's, to public figures.

Jacobson is a recognized thought leader in entrepreneurship and his book and video course, Navigating Entrepreneurship are used in business schools at colleges and universities. Through coaching, motivational speaking, and writing, he teaches the skills, traits and characteristics needed to achieve great accomplishments in one's business and personal life. In addition to the importance of having a vision and setting goals for achievement, he speaks with credibility from experience about leadership in managing fear, takings risks, decision-making, perseverance, and leading with passion.

A two-time TEDx speaker, Larry is one of the few highly trained speakers to become a Certified World Class Speaking Coach. By working with the best of the best, he has the skills and ability to train other speakers how to improve their public speaking skills and **Own The Stage**.

He is the creator of the online video training programs, **Navigating Entrepreneurship**, and **Sail Into Retirement**, the first self-guided training program for non-fiscal retirement planning. He recently published **What's Your Encore? A Step-by-Step Guide to Retiring With Purpose and Fulfillment (formerly Your Ideal Retirement Workbook).**

Larry has recently been awarded the coveted Retirement Catalyst Award by the Retirement Coaches Association, for opening new doors, creating new boundaries, influencing others, and being a major contributor to the field of non-fiscal Retirement Coaching. A California native, circumnavigator and adventurer, Larry Jacobson is an avid sailor with over 50,000 blue water miles under his keel. He authored the six-time award-winning memoir of his circumnavigation in the book, <u>**The Boy Behind the Gate**</u> and a children's middle grade reader, <u>**Let's Go!**</u> about the journey. He lives in the San Francisco Bay Area and welcomes new friends and inquiries at: <u>**https://larryjacobson.com**</u>

For information about how you can become a better communicator, visit
www.OwnTheStage.org